31243 00 464 0016

D1128629

GREAT
WORLD CUP
MOMENTS

Michael Hurley

Heinemann Library
Chicago, Illinois

www.heinemannraintree.com
Visit our website to find out more information about Heinemann-Raintree books.

To order:

☎ Phone 888-454-2279

💻 Visit www.heinemannraintree.com to browse our catalog and order online.

© 2010 Heinemann Library
an imprint of Capstone Global Library, LLC
Chicago, Illinois

All rights reserved. No part of this publication may be reproduced or transmitted in any form or by any means, electronic or mechanical, including photocopying, recording, taping, or any information storage and retrieval system, without permission in writing from the publisher.

Edited by Kate de Villiers, Catherine Clarke, and Megan Cotugno
Designed by Steve Mead and Ken Vale Graphic Design
Picture research by Hannah Taylor
Originated by Dot Gradations Ltd
Printed and bound in China by CTPS

14 13 12 11 10
10 9 8 7 6 5 4 3 2 1

Library of Congress Cataloging-in-Publication Data
Hurley, Michael, 1979-
  Great World Cup moments / Michael Hurley.
    p. cm. -- (The World Cup)
  Includes bibliographical references and index.
  ISBN 978-1-4329-3450-7 (hc)
  1. World Cup (Soccer) I. Title.
  GV943.49.H87 2009
  796.334668--dc22

                              2009005261

Acknowledgments
The author and publishers are grateful to the following for permission to reproduce copyright material: © KPT Power Photo **background image**; Action Images pp. **14** (Sporting Pictures), **17** (Richard Heathcote), **19** (Reuters/Pawel Kopczynski), **18** (Reuters/Enrique Marcarian), **25** (Reuters/Gary Hershorn); Corbis pp. **7** (© Bettmann), **20** (TempSport/© Jean-Yves Ruszniewski), **22** (Reuters/David W. Cerny); Getty Images pp. **4 & 5** (Alex Livesey), **6** (Popperfoto/Rolls Press), **10, 15 & 24** (Bob Thomas), **11** (AFP), **13** (Hulton Archive/Central Press), **21** (Popperfoto), **27** (AFP/John Macdougall); PA Photos pp. **8 & 9** (© Empics), **12** (AP), **16** (© Empics/Matthew Ashton), **23** (© Empics/Alpha); Shutterstock **background image** (© Nikola I).

Cover photograph of Italian players celebrating as Fabio Cannavaro lifts the World Cup trophy following victory in Berlin, Germany, July 9, 2006, reproduced with permission of Getty Images/Alex Livesey.

Every effort has been made to contact copyright holders of material reproduced in this book. Any omissions will be rectified in subsequent printings if notice is given to the publisher.

All the Internet addresses (URLs) given in this book were valid at the time of going to press. However, due to the dynamic nature of the Internet, some addresses may have changed, or sites may have changed or ceased to exist since publication. While the author and publisher regret any inconvenience this may cause readers, no responsibility for any such changes can be accepted by either the author or the publisher.

CONTENTS

Some words are shown in the text in bold, **like this**. You can find out what they mean by looking in the glossary on page 31.

THE WORLD CUP

The FIFA World Cup is the most important soccer **tournament** in the world. The first World Cup was held in 1930, in Uruguay, South America. Uruguay was chosen as the **host** because its team was the current Olympic soccer champion. Most of the teams that participated were from Central and South America. The United States also came.

Few European teams took part in the World Cup in Uruguay because traveling long distances was much more difficult in 1930 than it is today. The teams would not have traveled by plane. They would have had to go on a long and tiring sea journey. The only European teams to come were from Belgium, France, Romania, and Yugoslavia. Uruguay beat its South American neighbors Argentina in the first World Cup final, on July 30, 1930. It won the match 4–2.

World Cup 2010

The 2010 FIFA World Cup will be held in South Africa. It will be the first time that the tournament has been held on the African **continent**. The number of teams taking part in the World Cup has more than doubled since the first tournament. There will be 32 teams competing in South Africa in 2010, compared to 13 in Uruguay in 1930.

Italy celebrates winning the 2006 World Cup. It beat France in the final.

In the past, teams were invited to play in the World Cup. Today, they have to qualify for the right to be involved. The only team that does not have to qualify is the team of the host nation.

Goals galore

Both of the World Cup semifinal matches in 1930 ended with the same incredible score: 6–1. Argentina beat the United States, and Uruguay beat Yugoslavia.

Since the **FIFA** World Cup began, many great matches have been played. Some of these matches have involved great individual performances or **controversial** incidents. The greatest matches are often the semifinals and finals, because there is so much at stake!

England vs. West Germany, 1966

The 1966 World Cup was held in England. It was the first time that England had **hosted** the world's most important soccer **tournament**, and the players and the public were very excited.

The players from England lined up in red shirts on the day of the final. They were slight favorites over West Germany, whose players wore white and black. It was a close match that ended 2–2 in normal time, after Germany tied in the 89th minute! The England team showed great strength physically and mentally to keep playing well in **extra time**. Alan Ball, the England **midfielder**, was inspirational to his teammates, and England again started to look like the favorite for the title.

Stolen!

In the build-up to the final, the official World Cup trophy was stolen. It was found by a dog out walking with his owner in a London park. The dog, named Pickles, became an instant hero with the English public.

Controversial goal

England scored a controversial goal in extra time to make the score 3–2. Geoff Hurst, who had tied the score at 1–1 earlier in the game, managed to hit a shot past the West German goalkeeper. His shot hit the crossbar and bounced down. England's players immediately began celebrating a goal as the referee and linesman discussed whether the goal should stand. They decided that the ball had crossed the goal line: it was a goal.

STATS

TEAMS: ENGLAND, WEST GERMANY

DATE: JULY 30, 1966

VENUE: WEMBLEY STADIUM, LONDON, ENGLAND

ATTENDANCE: 93,000

FINAL SCORE: 2–2, AET 4–2

The players on the England team, with the huge crowd in Wembley Stadium behind them, knew that they just needed to keep the score as it was to be world champions. In the closing seconds of the game, England's captain, Bobby Moore, played a long ball out from defense. Geoff Hurst latched onto the ball, ran past the West German defense, and took a shot. It was a goal, a **hat trick** for Hurst. The score was 4–2, the match was over, and England had won the World Cup final.

Italy vs. Brazil, 1970

The 1970 **FIFA** World Cup final has been described by many as the greatest soccer match of all time. One reason for this was a clash of playing styles. The team from Brazil was full of skill and flair. The Italians were strong, solid, and reliable.

The majority of fans in the stadium wanted Brazil to win. Everyone liked the way that the team played soccer: with quick, **incisive** passing and **midfielders** who had speed and amazing **dribbling** skills. Added to this, of course, the team had soccer **legend** Pelé. This was to be his last World Cup appearance, and many fans wanted to see him lift the trophy for the third time in his career.

STATS

TEAMS: BRAZIL, ITALY

DATE: JUNE 21, 1970

VENUE: AZTECA STADIUM, MEXICO CITY, MEXICO

ATTENDANCE: 107,412

FINAL SCORE: 4–1

At the time of the 1970 World Cup, Pelé was the greatest soccer player in the world.

In the World Cup final, Italy could not match the amazing soccer skills of the team from Brazil.

Brazilian magic

The team from Brazil started the match slightly better than the Italians. It had a few chances to score before Pelé put it 1–0 ahead in the 18th minute. This early goal seemed to make Brazil relax too much. Italy managed to get through the Brazilian defense and score. At halftime the score was level at 1–1.

Color TV

The 1970 World Cup final was the first to be shown on television in color.

In the second half, both teams tried to control the match, but it was the individual talents of the Brazilian players that made the difference. The Brazil midfielder Gerson scored following a neat passing move involving four different players. Brazil had the advantage, 2–1. Five minutes later Pelé headed a **cross** into the path of Jairzinho. He squeezed his shot past the Italian goalkeeper, to a score of 3–1.

Brazil had victory in its sights, but there were still several minutes left to play. Brazil's players began to really enjoy themselves. They passed the ball effortlessly around. Brazil scored again! Carlos Alberto received the ball from Pelé, and without breaking stride he struck his shot powerfully into the goal. Brazil had won the World Cup.

West Germany vs. France, 1982

The 1982 semifinal between West Germany and France was a fascinating match between two of the giants of European soccer. France had the edge in terms of **technique**. In Michel Platini and Alain Giresse it had players who could win a match with one amazing pass or move. West Germany, in contrast, was well organized and determined. This was perhaps France's best chance to win the World Cup so far. Although West Germany had been successful in previous **tournaments**, the French were expected to win here.

STATS

TEAMS: WEST GERMANY, FRANCE

DATE: JULY 8, 1982

VENUE: SANCHEZ PIZJUAN STADIUM, SEVILLE, SPAIN

ATTENDANCE: 70,000

FINAL SCORE: 3–3 AET, 5–4 PENS

Early in the match France was frustrated by the Germans' defensive **tactics**. Germany's **defenders** and **midfielders** made it hard for France to score. West Germany scored the opening goal of the match. Platini then tied the score from a **penalty** to make it 1–1 at halftime.

Michel Platini (in blue) plays at the 1982 World Cup semifinal vs. West Germany.

Shocking decision

Early in the second half, West Germany's goalkeeper, Toni Schumacher, came rushing out of his area to tackle one of France's players. The Frenchman, Patrick Battiston, clashed with the goalkeeper and was left on the ground, unconscious. The French players and fans were horrified that the referee did not eject Schumacher. No more goals were scored in the second half, so the game went to **extra time**.

This photograph was taken just before the shocking collision between Toni Schumacher (right) and Patrick Battiston. As you can see in this photo, the ball had gone past the goalkeeper.

Both teams knew that a **penalty shoot-out** awaited them if they could not win the match in extra time. After scoring two goals in the first half of extra time, France looked as though it would go on to the final. West Germany, however, was very determined and managed to score another two goals to make the score 3–3. This meant a penalty shoot-out was needed.

West Germany won the shoot-out 5–4. Its goalkeeper, Schumacher, saved two of the French penalties. The players from France were devastated. After being 3–1 up in extra time, they had lost. West Germany had fought hard to make it to the final.

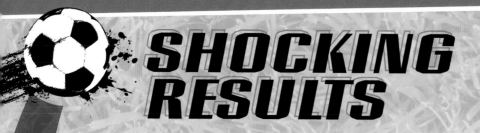

SHOCKING RESULTS

In addition to great matches, the **FIFA** World Cup has also seen some shocking results. The most shocking results are often when an **inferior** team beats a well-established soccer nation.

Brazil vs. Uruguay, 1950

Brazil was the favorite in the final of the 1950 World Cup. It was considered to be the greatest team in the world at the time. It had scored 13 goals in its previous two matches at the World Cup and was playing on home soil. Over 170,000 people packed into the Maracana stadium to watch their team play Uruguay. Millions of people were at home listening to the match on the radio and preparing to celebrate after the final whistle.

STATS

TEAMS: BRAZIL, URUGUAY

DATE: JULY 16, 1950

VENUE: MARACANA STADIUM, RIO DE JANEIRO, BRAZIL

ATTENDANCE: 174,000

FINAL SCORE: 1–2

Uruguay beats Brazil in front of packed crowds at the Maracana stadium in July 1950.

Uruguay had other ideas. Although its team was not as good as Brazil's, it certainly deserved its place in the final. Brazil took the lead at the beginning of the second half, but could not increase on this advantage. When Uruguay tied the score, the stadium fell silent. When it scored again, it felt as though the whole of Brazil went quiet. Shocked, the Brazilians failed to get back into the match, and Uruguay became world champion.

North Korea vs. Italy, 1966

Perhaps one of the biggest World Cup shocks was when North Korea knocked Italy out of the World Cup in 1966. It beat Italy 1–0. North Korea had never played in a World Cup before. Italy, one of the pre-**tournament** favorites, had to beat North Korea to go on to the second round. It was expected to win comfortably. The North Koreans had nothing to lose. After scoring before halftime, North Korea managed to hold out for a famous victory that embarrassed the Italians.

STATS

TEAMS: NORTH KOREA, ITALY

DATE: JULY 19, 1966

VENUE: AYRESOME PARK, MIDDLESBROUGH, ENGLAND

ATTENDANCE: 20,000

FINAL SCORE: 1–0

The winning goal! This shot that went past goalkeeper Enrico Albertosi sent Italy out of the 1966 World Cup.

West Germany vs. Algeria, 1982

In 1982 Algeria was playing in its first World Cup. West Germany, a winner in 1974, was one of the favorites for the 1982 **tournament** held in Spain. After a goalless first half, Algeria took the lead in the 54th minute. The Germans had underestimated the Algerians and now needed to play much better to win the game. Karl-Heinz Rummenigge, one of the most famous German players, managed to score a goal. Within a minute Algeria had shocked its **opponents** again by scoring, to make the score 2–1. Algeria held out for an incredible victory.

STATS

TEAMS: WEST GERMANY, ALGERIA

DATE: JUNE 16, 1982

VENUE: EL MOLINON, GIJON, SPAIN

ATTENDANCE: 42,000

FINAL SCORE: 1–2

World Cup runner-up

Luckily for West Germany it managed to recover from the shocking result against Algeria. The team made it all the way to the final, where it was beaten by Italy.

Algerian players are overjoyed to beat West Germany.

Cameroon teammates pile on top of Omam Biyick in celebration, after his goal against Argentina.

Argentina vs. Cameroon, 1990

The opening match of each World Cup often involves the winner of the previous tournament. Argentina won the World Cup in 1986, and so played Cameroon in the opening match of the 1990 World Cup in Italy. Because it had won the last World Cup, Argentina was one of the favorites to win in 1990. Cameroon had never won a World Cup match before, tying all three matches in its previous World Cup appearance.

STATS

TEAMS: ARGENTINA, CAMEROON

DATE: JUNE 8, 1990

VENUE: STADIO GIUSEPPE MEAZZA SAN SIRO, MILAN, ITALY

ATTENDANCE: 73,780

FINAL SCORE: 0–1

When Cameroon took the lead midway through the second half, it looked as if there was going to be a major shock. Despite having two players ejected, Cameroon had the determination to hold off Argentina's attacks. Cameroon had achieved the best result in its history, with a 1–0 win.

United States vs. Iran, 1998

The United States and Iran were not favorites to win the World Cup in 1998. However, the United States expected to be able to beat Iran in a **group match** and move to the next round. Iran had not won a match in its previous World Cup appearance in 1978. Most **spectators** did not think it had much of a chance against the United States.

STATS

TEAMS: UNITED STATES, IRAN

DATE: JUNE 21, 1998

VENUE: STADE GERLAND, LYON, FRANCE

ATTENDANCE: 39,100

FINAL SCORE: 1–2

The players from Iran worked harder on the field and took a two-goal lead. The United States scored a goal in the final few minutes. But Iran won the match 2–1. This result made headlines all around the world.

Before the match, most people thought that the United States would easily beat Iran.

Trouble off the field

Because of **political tension** between the two nations, the **FIFA** World Cup match between the United States and Iran had more significance than usual. The winners would be able to use the result to show that they had superiority over the other, at least on the soccer field.

France vs. Senegal, 2002

The match between France and Senegal was the opening match of the 2002 World Cup. France had won the **tournament** on home soil in 1998 and was expected to do well again. This was Senegal's first match in a World Cup. Most spectators expected an easy win for France. They thought the Senegal team had some promising young players, but that France had more experience.

STATS

TEAMS: FRANCE, SENEGAL

DATE: MAY 31, 2002

VENUE: SEOUL WORLD CUP STADIUM, SEOUL, SOUTH KOREA

ATTENDANCE: 62,561

FINAL SCORE: 0–1

The Senegal team had to play without fear if it was to stand a chance of winning, and it did this superbly. Although France had more **possession** and more shots, it was Senegal that managed to score. The team held on for an amazing result. France did not recover from this result and failed to make it to the second round of the World Cup. The confidence gained from this result helped the Senegal team to play well in the tournament. It made it all the way to the quarterfinals.

The players from France (in blue) are devastated after being beaten by Senegal.

Since the **FIFA** World Cup began in 1930, there have been 2,063 goals scored in the 18 **tournaments** (up to 2006). Whether the goals come from **free kicks**, **penalties**, own goals, headers, long range, or tap-ins, they all count. Some of the goals scored have been spectacular.

Esteban Cambiasso (Argentina) vs. Serbia and Montenegro, 2006

This goal is considered by many fans to be the greatest goal since Carlos Alberto's goal for Brazil in 1970 (see page 21). The standard of play in the World Cup is usually very high. **Possession** of the ball is very important. During this **group match**, Argentina taught its **opponents** a lesson about keeping possession of the ball.

The ball was passed between teammates more than 20 times before it reached Cambiasso. He traded passes with Hernan Crespo just inside the 18-yard box. Cambiasso was left with the task of putting the ball into the goal. He placed his shot to the left of the goalkeeper, into the net. It was an incredible goal.

Cambiasso's shot flies past the goalkeeper to finish off a great move by Argentina.

This photo was taken just before Michael Owen scored his amazing World Cup goal.

Michael Owen (England) vs. Argentina, 1998

Playing in his first World Cup, Michael Owen was only 18 when he scored a great goal. David Beckham played a simple **through-ball** to Owen just inside the Argentina half. Owen used his speed and agility to glide past a couple of Argentina **defenders**. Then he smashed his shot past the goalkeeper from just inside the penalty area. From this point on, everyone knew who Michael Owen was. He had announced his soccer talent to the world.

Using his speed and skill, Maradona dribbles the ball past several England players, before scoring his incredible goal.

Diego Maradona (Argentina) vs. England, 1986

One of the greatest goals ever scored in a World Cup **tournament** was in the 1986 match between Argentina and England. Diego Maradona scored both his team's goals when Argentina beat England 2–1.

Although there was **controversy** about Maradona's first goal, the second one was simply amazing. He received the ball inside the Argentina half and quickly got past two England players. Using his natural balance and skill with the ball, he began to move into the England half. With a burst of speed he **dribbled** the ball past two England **defenders**, and into the England **penalty** area.

After taking the ball past five players, Maradona then took the ball past England's goalkeeper. When another desperate attempt to steal the ball came, he used his strength to hold off the challenge. He shot the ball into the net. It was an amazing goal and an incredible achievement!

Carlos Alberto (Brazil) vs. Italy, 1970

The last goal in the final of the 1970 World Cup is regarded by many fans as the greatest goal scored in World Cup history. Brazil was already beating Italy 3–1, and the Italians appeared to have accepted defeat. With five minutes left to go it looked as though Brazil was going to play it safe and keep **possession** of the ball. Brazilian teams, however, love to entertain and score goals.

Clodoaldo took control of the ball from a teammate near the halfway line and breezed past four Italians. He passed the ball out to the left to Tostao. Tostao played a long pass directly to Jairzinho. Picking the ball up wide on the left of the field, Jairzinho began running at the Italian defense. He passed the ball to Pelé a few yards outside the penalty area.

Effortlessly, Pelé rolled the ball to his right, just inside the **opponents'** penalty area. Carlos Alberto had moved forward from his defensive position. Without breaking stride he smashed the ball into the goal. It flew past the Italian goalkeeper, who had no chance of stopping it. It was an amazing team goal and a fitting end to a great match.

Carlos Alberto celebrates his goal for Brazil in its 4–1 win over Italy.

PENALTY HEARTACHES

After the **group stages** of the **FIFA** World Cup, **penalty shoot-outs** are used to decide the winner of a match that has ended in a tie. After the standard 90 minutes of play, if the score is tied, 30 minutes of **extra time** are played. If the score is still tied after that, a penalty shoot-out is used. Each team has five **penalties**, and the winner is the team that ends the shoot-out with the most goals. After five penalties each, if it is still a tie, then "sudden death" penalties are taken. Sudden death penalties mean that both teams take turns to take penalties until one of the teams misses and the other team scores, winning the match.

Many famous World Cup matches have been won or lost using a penalty shoot-out. This can be an agonizing way of leaving a **tournament** for players and supporters if their team loses.

A saved penalty can be the difference between winning or losing a match. Holland's goalkeeper, Van Der Sar, has just saved this penalty.

France vs. Brazil, 1986 quarterfinal

In this quarterfinal match the score at the end of extra time was 1–1. Brazil was expected to win the match and was the favorite for the World Cup. Socrates, one of Brazil's all-time greatest players, took Brazil's first penalty. His penalty was saved by the French goalkeeper, Joel Bats. Bats had also saved a penalty during the match. Both teams scored their next three penalties. Michel Platini, of France, missed the target completely when it came to his turn. The score in the shoot-out was 3–3.

STATS

TEAMS: FRANCE, BRAZIL

DATE: JUNE 21, 1986

VENUE: JALISCO STADIUM, GUADALAJARA, MEXICO

ATTENDANCE: 65,000

FINAL SCORE: 1–1 AET, 4–3 PENS

Michel Platini is devastated after missing his penalty against Brazil.

Julio Cesar took Brazil's fifth penalty, but his effort hit the post and bounced away from the goal. Luis Fernandez had the chance to win the match for France. He coolly placed his shot into the corner of the net. France had knocked out the World Cup favorites.

West Germany vs. England, 1990 semifinal

This semifinal match was the farthest England had gone at a World Cup since it won the trophy in 1966. West Germany had not won the World Cup since 1974.

An entertaining match ended 1–1 after **extra time**. Both teams scored their first three **penalties**. When Stuart Pearce stepped up to take England's fourth penalty, his team was very close to appearing in its second-ever World Cup final. Unfortunately for England, the West German goalkeeper, Bodo Illgner, guessed which way to go.

STATS

TEAMS: WEST GERMANY, ENGLAND

DATE: JULY 4, 1990

VENUE: STADIO DELLE ALPI, TURIN, ITALY

ATTENDANCE: 62,628

FINAL SCORE: 1–1 AET, 4–3 PENS

West Germany's goalkeeper, Bodo Illgner, uses his legs to save Stuart Pearce's powerfully struck penalty.

West Germany took advantage and scored its next penalty. This meant England had to score its last penalty. Chris Waddle stepped up. He had to score his penalty to keep England in the match. The pressure showed as he shot his penalty wildly over the crossbar.

Brazil vs. Italy, 1994 final

The 1994 World Cup final was played between two of the most successful teams in the history of the **tournament**. Brazil had last won the trophy in 1970. Italy had last won the tournament in 1982.

Neither Brazil nor Italy had managed to score during the match or in extra time. The only way to separate them would be a **penalty shoot-out**. Italy had a bad start. Franco Baresi missed the target with his penalty. But Brazil could not take advantage. Marcio Santos's penalty was saved. Both teams scored their next two penalties. Italy's next penalty was saved by Brazil's goalkeeper, Taffarel. Brazil scored its next penalty.

STATS

TEAMS: BRAZIL, ITALY

DATE: JULY 17, 1994

VENUE: ROSE BOWL, LOS ANGELES, CALIFORNIA

ATTENDANCE: 94,194

FINAL SCORE: 0–0 AET, 3–2 PENS

The score was 3–2 when Italy's Roberto Baggio stepped up. Most **spectators** expected him to score easily from the penalty spot. Baggio blazed his shot over the crossbar. The Brazilians began to celebrate.

Roberto Baggio's penalty flies over the goal and misses. This meant that Brazil won its fourth World Cup.

WORLD CUP MADNESS

The **FIFA** World Cup is very popular with fans all around the world. The **tournament** offers people a chance to watch great players, teams, matches, and goals. Sometimes fans also get to see moments of madness.

Diego Maradona's "Hand of God"

Diego Maradona is one of the greatest players to have played in the World Cup. He had amazing **dribbling** skills. He also had incredible balance and vision on the field.

During the 1986 World Cup in Mexico, Diego Maradona scored an amazing goal (see page 20). In the same match against England he also scored a goal that should not have been allowed. He used his hand to punch the ball into the goal. If you are not the goalkeeper you cannot use your hands to move the ball if you are on the field. The referee did not see what happened, and the goal was allowed. England lost the match 2–1.

The players from the England team and their fans were angry. They could not believe the decision to allow the goal. When he was asked about what happened, Maradona said that he was proud to have scored a goal this way. He called it the "Hand of God." Argentina went on to win the World Cup in 1986. Maradona was named player of the tournament.

Zinedine Zidane's head butt

It was the 2006 World Cup final in Germany. France's captain and most important player, Zinedine Zidane, was trying to help his team beat Italy.

In **extra time** Italy **defender** Marco Materazzi appeared to say something to Zidane. Zidane reacted by suddenly head butting Materazzi hard in the chest. Materazzi fell to the ground. The referee had no option but to eject Zidane. It was his last appearance at the World Cup. It was also his last appearance for France. France had to play the last few minutes of the match with only 10 players. It held out for **penalties**, but lost to Italy in the **penalty shoot-out**.

Italy's Marco Materazzi falls to the ground after being head butted by France's Zinedine Zidane.

WORLD CUP STATS

World Cup tournaments

Year	Host	Winner	Runner-up	Score
1930	Uruguay	Uruguay	Argentina	4–2
1934	Italy	Italy	Czechoslovakia	2–1 AET
1938	France	Italy	Hungary	4–2
1950	Brazil	Uruguay	Brazil	2–1
1954	Switzerland	West Germany	Hungary	3–2
1958	Sweden	Brazil	Sweden	5–2
1962	Chile	Brazil	Czechoslovakia	3–1
1966	England	England	West Germany	4–2 AET
1970	Mexico	Brazil	Italy	4–1
1974	West Germany	West Germany	Holland	2–1
1978	Argentina	Argentina	Holland	3–1 AET
1982	Spain	Italy	West Germany	3–1
1986	Mexico	Argentina	West Germany	3–2
1990	Italy	West Germany	Argentina	1–0
1994	United States	Brazil	Italy	(0–0 AET) 3–2 PENS
1998	France	France	Brazil	3–0
2002	S. Korea/Japan	Brazil	Germany	2–0
2006	Germany	Italy	France	(1–1 AET) 5–3 PENS

World Cup records

World Cup appearances

The record for the most World Cup appearances is held by Germany's Lothar Matthaus. He has played in 25 World Cup matches.

World Cup goals

Brazil's Ronaldo holds the record for the most goals scored in World Cup history. He has scored 15 goals. The record for the most goals scored in one **tournament** is held by France's Just Fontaine. He scored an amazing 13 goals in 1958.

The fastest goal

The fastest goal ever scored in a World Cup match was scored by Turkey's Hakan Suker against South Korea in 2002. It took only 11 seconds for Sukur to score!

Red card record

The World Cup record that no player wants is the one for the quickest **red card** in World Cup history. This record is held by Uruguay's Jose Batista, who was ejected against Scotland in 1986 after only 56 seconds!

Highest attendance

The highest attendance in World Cup history is 174,000. This record was set in 1950 when Brazil played Uruguay in the World Cup final at the Maracana Stadium in Rio de Janeiro, Brazil.

Books to read

Beckham, David. *Beckham: Both Feet on the Ground.* New York: HarperCollins, 2003.

Buckley, Jr., James. *Pelé.* New York: Dorling Kindersley, 2007.

Collie, Ashley Jude. *World of Soccer: A Complete Guide to the World's Most Popular Sport.* New York: Rosen, 2003.

Gifford, Clive. *Soccer: The Ultimate Guide to the Beautiful Game.* Boston: Kingfisher, 2004.

Godsall, Ben. *The Making of a Champion: An International Soccer Star.* Chicago: Heinemann Library, 2005.

Lineker, Gary. *Soccer.* New York: Dorling Kindersley, 2005.

Savage, Jeff. *Amazing Athletes: David Beckham.* Minneapolis: Lerner, 2000.

Shea, Therese. *Greatest Sports Heroes: Soccer Stars.* New York: Children's Press, 2007.

Websites

www.fifa.com
This website has all of the information about the FIFA World Cup. It is great for finding out about your favorite players and teams.

www.ussoccer.com
This is the official website of the U.S. Soccer Federation. It provides news and coverage of all the U.S. teams and players.

GLOSSARY

continent   one of the world's largest landmasses. There are seven continents on Earth.

controversy   argument or difference of opinion

cross   when the ball is kicked from the side of the field to the area in front of the goal

defender   position of a soccer player on the field. Defenders try to stop the opposition from scoring.

dribble   run with the ball at your feet

extra time   extra period of play that is added on to a soccer match if it is a tie at the end of normal time (90 minutes). Extra time lasts for 30 minutes, with two halves of 15 minutes.

FIFA   (*Fédération International de Football* [Soccer] *Association*) international organization responsible for soccer around the world

free kick   kick of the ball awarded by the referee after a foul

group match   a match in the group stage, when teams play each other to decide who will move on to the next stage

group stage   stage in a tournament when teams play in groups to decide who will move on to the next stage

hat trick   when a single player scores three goals in a soccer match

host   team holding an event in its own country

incisive   quick and skilled passing of the ball

inferior   less successful than. An inferior team will have won fewer tournaments than a superior, more successful one.

legend   extremely famous person who is well known for his or her particular talent or success

midfielder   player or players positioned in the middle of the field who link the attacking and defending players

opponent   person or team that you are playing against

penalty   the referee gives a penalty if a foul happens in the penalty area, an 18-yard rectangular area surrounding the goal. The ball is placed on a spot 12 yards from the goal, and only the goalkeeper is allowed to stop the shot.

penalty shoot-out   after extra time, if the scores are still tied, the two teams pick five players from each team to try to score five penalties. The team that scores the most penalties wins.

political tension   unease and disagreement between two countries

possession   keeping the ball with your team

red card   card shown by the referee to a player, usually for a dangerous foul. The player leaves the field, and the team continues with just 10 players.

spectator   person watching a match

tactics   way in which a team plans to play, agreed upon between the players and their coach

technique   way of doing something. Different players control the ball in different ways on the soccer field, and there is good and bad technique for certain passes and skills.

through-ball   pass beyond the opposition's defense that creates a goal-scoring opportunity

tournament   organized number of matches that lead to a final. The winner of the final game wins the tournament.

INDEX